# True Wealth
# Is Empowered

# True Wealth Is Empowered

# Table Of Contents

# Foreword

Building wealth is not magic. There's a lot more common sense, inspired action and logic involved in building wealth than most "gurus" claim. It's a lot more about systems and a lot less about ostensible "secrets". There are plenty of good simple genuine moneymaking opportunities accessible if you search for them, but make sure to investigate each one thoroughly first. Find out how successful and reputable the people offering it are. Get all the info you need here.

# Empowered True Wealth

# Chapter 1:

*Basics on Wealth*

---

# Synopsis

Don't fall victim to "I was able to make six figures within 24 hours" kinds of claims. Even though you can become rich quite quickly – six figures in one year or less is really possible – it still takes preparation, education, action and practice. You need to exercise your psychological muscles and mind as well as apply what you discover, if you're to become successful as a wealth builder.

# The Basics

Good thing is that it's quite easy to do it right. To get started, consider learning from those who've already achieved success in the area you're interested in. Investigate and learn how they built riches and seek ways to copy their efforts yourself. The more you discover and the more successful you become, the more you can think of new ideas and expand on your own.

As you can see, regardless of the wealth building strategies you apply, you have to follow a logical process like building a home, for instance. Build a solid foundation, begin small and create your wealth progressively. As you earn more money, you can re-invest it in your sales efforts, business and investments to keep a stable economic base.

When you first begin to earn more money, it can be enticing to spend it on other stuff, but it's important to apply discipline at this point.

Keep in mind that without a strong foundation, your financial house won't stand, no matter how beautiful the accessories, furnishings or the paint job might be. The same goes to the investment portfolio or business.

Use some of your new riches for fun, but put most of it in your wealth building system. The more you do this, your financial house will grow quicker and the sooner you will build major wealth.

Building wealth is all about planning and knowledge. With enough preparation, you can be on your way to your financial freedom. It is not reserved for workaholics or entrepreneurial masterminds.

Building wealth is a course based on systems and these systems can be learned and used by anyone who believes in himself and has the desire to succeed. Although it's a learned skill and a lifelong practice, once you follow through, you'll start seeing results almost instantly.

Building wealth is not only for the rich. Always remember that you are just as worthy of vast wealth as any billionaire or millionaire in the world.

You deserve to be wealthy and you are more than capable of building as much as you need and want and more. As soon as you see things from that perspective and really trust it, a new universe of possibilities and abundance opens up for you!

# Chapter 2:

## *The Uncertainty of Global Economics*

# Synopsis

Some politicians and economists argue that the 2 years of harsh times which visited the U.S. and euro area throughout the Great Recession of 2008-2009 should've been followed by quick recoveries. Late Nobel Prize winner economist Milton Friedman referred to this as the guitar string recession theory. When a guitar string is pulled down and then released, it bounces back. The more it's pulled down, the quicker it returns.

# About Economics

On the other hand, lots of highly developed economies ever since the Great Recession have not followed this idea. Instead, the deep recession in those economies was followed by recoveries which have been disappointingly slow and weak. It's like the string was pulled down very hard that it snapped.

These growths are somewhat of a mystery. Why has the present recovery been very slow? Some argue that recoveries after economic crises have a tendency to be slow as the legacy of the crisis (weak credit expansion, persistent issues in housing markets and balance sheet repair) weighs on movement. This argument definitely has its merits, taking into account the historical record.

On the other hand, the current recovery has been different at any rate in one significant dimension from the previous ones, whether related to economic crises or not. It has suffered bouts of high uncertainty. This suggests a corresponding explanation for the weak recovery, one that highlights the functions played by policy and macroeconomic uncertainty in limiting economic activity.

Businesses have been unsure about the regulatory and fiscal environment in Europe and U.S. and this apprehension of an indecipherable future has possibly been one of the issues leading them to push back hiring and investment. This is clearly demonstrated in a survey in the U.S. by the National Association for

Business Economic, which showed that the majority of a group of 236 business economists feels that uncertainty about financial policy is delaying the speed of economic recovery. How significant is uncertainty in motivating economic activity? What are the main aspects of uncertainty and its impact on economic recovery?

Economic uncertainty pertains to an environment wherein little or nothing is identified about the economy's future condition. There are various causes of economic uncertainty including different outlooks about growth prospects, changes in financial and economic policies, acts of terrorism, productivity movements, natural disasters and wars. Although uncertainty is hard to quantify, recent research has been capable of developing different measures using various approaches.

The ongoing recovery in highly developed economies has coincided with substandard cumulative growth in investment and consumption together with a sharp and continued reduction in investment in structures because uncertainty has remained elevated.

Historically, high uncertainty coincides with periods of substandard growth. The recent increase in uncertainty boosts the possibility of another global recession.

It's hard for policymakers to beat the inherent uncertainty economies usually faced over the business cycle. On the other hand, uncertainty about economic policy is abnormally high and it seems to contribute drastically to macroeconomic uncertainty. By executing bold and appropriate measures, policymakers can lessen policy-induced uncertainty. In turn, this can help start economic development in the euro area and reinforce the recovery in the U.S.

# Chapter 3:

*What Is True Wealth?*

---

# Synopsis

Wealth is usually associated with money, but this isn't the whole picture. Even though financial security is a good sign of wealth, it's not true wealth's only dimension. Actually, measuring true wealth just through monetary terms can be confusing. Money is definitely an important part of modern life, but there are other equally crucial aspects of living that should be considered when talking about true wealth. True wealth goes beyond the idea of financial stability or material abundance.

# True Wealth

Wealth is a way of feeling and being in the world. It means that you have abundance in every area of life. People are meant to live a life of profusion. There's an evil rumor in the mind that there's not enough for everyone. There's not enough money, not enough food or not enough of everything you can imagine. This is a complete lie because there's enough.

There's more than enough for everybody. The problem is that people have been taught that there's lack in the world. You see people who don't have what they want and they conclude that wealth is a faraway place that's very hard to reach. This is certainly far from the reality.

There's more than enough wealth in every area for each person to have everything he or she wants and more. Everyone wants to find someone to love or perhaps you already have found your special someone. Is there a limit on love? Sometimes, people will put limits on love, but that's not true love. True love has no restraints, it's boundless and it's limitless. It can be given all the time and never run out. Everything else is the same. Wealth is profuse and people should learn to see that there's more than enough for everyone.

Wealth is having profusion in your relationships. It's having family, loved ones and friends and great relationships with them that bring happiness to people's lives every day. These are mutually valuable relationships that are indeed a two way road. Without healthy relationships, life can be very stressful and hard. Wealth in relationships is all about both of you obtaining more than you put in. Health is wealth and this is true.

Having lots of money, but not being fit enough to enjoy it isn't true wealth. There are many people who'd give their entire fortune for better relationships and better health.

On the other hand, there are poor people who have great health and great relationships. This is most likely as close to wealth as people can get until they can take care of their financial state. True wealth is about abundance in relationships, finances and health.

Wealth has one more area – the realm of spirituality. Some people feel rich in the realm of spirituality when they're able to go to church regularly and give to God. Others feel rich when they have a reason to dedicate themselves to.

You have to decide what true wealth in every area means to you and understand that you don't just deserve it, but can also have it. You can have the love, relationships, health, money and things you want. There's more than enough available for everyone.

# Chapter 4:

*What Is The Empowered Wealth Mindset?*

# Synopsis

Have you ever questioned why some people seem to be very lucky and enjoying a great life while others are not? Can a person change his life and escape the situation he's in right now at once? How can one get all the things he has always wanted? Is there a secret on how to attain all these? What is the empowered wealth mindset and how can you achieve it?

# The Mindset

The truth is that the mind can do much more than you can possibly think of. Unfortunately, most people just do not have the motivation and the initiative to believe and know their potentials. They're not aware of the control that they have over the mind. Most people have not realized that they could actually gain control of their mindset and focus their thinking on changing the direction of their lives to a better path and achieve wealth.

So, what is the secret in order for you to gain control over your mindset so that you can effectively take conscious efforts as well as achieve authority over your life? First of all, you have to learn and practice complete responsibility of your actions and the choices you make. No matter what the circumstances may be as a result of your actions and choices, you must learn and accept your mistakes, but refuse to get affected so that you can stand up and take a new direction to achieve your goals.

To achieve an empowered wealth mindset and effectively attract money into your life, you shouldn't stop learning and finding new ways to keep on growing intellectually. This is the reason why you are able to attain balance in your life by the way you think and perceive opportunities that provide the avenue for you to build wealth and enjoy a comfortable life.

Empower your mind and yourself so that you can develop a wealth mindset. Here are some of the time-tested plans proven by well-off people to get you true financial freedom.

- Do not spend more than you make. Only spend for stuff that you really need and invest or save the rest. Investing should be done wisely and carefully. Make sure that your investments earn.
- Believe in the Law of Attraction. Think of money, think wealthy and get rid of all disempowering ideas you have about yourself and money.
- Get rid of your debts if you want to be wealthy. If you're currently paying off a certain loan, pay it off quick.
- Buy assets to raise your net worth. It might be in the form of bonds, shares of stocks, business venture or real estate. Be sure to gain assets that you can fund.

Live a sensible life every day by counting each cent coming out of your pocket. Simple and small things that you can give up make a great difference and this would mean extra savings. In general, empowered wealth mindset is about thinking that you can become wealthy and you deserve to be well-off. The empowered wealth mindset can help you effectively attract money into your life so that you can live the kind of life you have always wanted!

# Chapter 5:

## *Traditional Planning vs. New Age Ideas*

# Synopsis

Traditional business planning involves getting the market research properly before anything else is done. Problem is how do you research new?

By definition, innovation, the foundation of the entrepreneur's actions, is something that doesn't currently exist. What was the desktop computer market's size when Bill Gates made a decision to put one on each desk? He saw what didn't exist that is why it's impossible to investigate and document. In addition, entrepreneurial opportunities usually emerge in markets of great change and turbulence making it almost impossible for things to remain still long enough to be investigated.

Entrepreneurs get their best market research from starting in a semi-test approach and adjusting to the market as it reacts to their new endeavor's offer.

# New Ideas

The traditional business plan also asks you to sit down as well as plan out the next three to five years and explain carefully the developing series of events. Those who have actually started several new ventures know that you're flat out getting the first three to five months properly, let alone the next three to five years.

Experienced entrepreneurs understand that there are just a lot of variables in resources, product development, market acceptances and the entrepreneur themselves to predict comprehensively and meaningfully the traditional three to five years business plan's outlook. Experienced entrepreneurs will trust more in their capability to adjust to the changing environment instead of implementing the comprehensive instructions of a prepared plan basically made in ignorance.

Besides, opportunities won't wait. It's going to take you around three to six months to create a traditional business plan. Now, if your opportunity is ready to wait around for you, then good, but more than likely, that opportunity you're researching has already been taken advantage of by another entrepreneur who realized that timing was everything. They know that the window of opportunity is extremely fleeting and without the pro-active and timely action, it's lost forever.

If you're a serious candidate for launching a new business enterprise and not only a dreamer, then in some way you already have a business launch that's in play with your trial offers to in-house consumers and your prototypes. The majority of entrepreneurial text books agree that more than 70 percent of successful entrepreneurial ventures are started by present domain experts who've directly experienced a particular problem for which they've come up with an excellent solution.

They don't rely on the traditional plan that much as they are more than likely to employ their insider knowledge, strategic alliances and experience to firstly assess the opportunity and take it to market through their extremely accessible distribution channels.

There's also very little flexibility in traditional business plans. It's introduced as a one-size-fits-all when obviously, it doesn't.

Traditional planning is a corporate tool basically made under a risk avoidance mindset, which is the opposite of what an entrepreneur's viewpoint in the planning process is. The latter's outlook is from a risk management one.

The simplicity of business entry through the internet has made the price of being mistaken of little consequence. Through online marketing, business websites and other new age ideas, services and products can be tested and tried before any major commitment of resources. This permits entrepreneurs to modify their business model to meet market demands and needs.

A lot of new business enterprise hopefuls focus on making the perfect business plan wherein they should be focusing on making the perfect cash flow. There are far more credible methods that they could adopt such as a website gathering email addresses of customers interested in your products or services, customer testimonials and lists and prototypes already within the market under limited release.

It's also very possible that the planning process is in fact counter-productive for the entrepreneur as it can create a paralysis from too much investigation. What is needed and what most thriving entrepreneurs provide is action – making what they want happen.

Now, smart entrepreneurs, while agreeing to reduce the importance of writing a traditional business plan, won't abandon the planning process all at once. They'll just approach it from an outlook that best conveys the way in which they expand and take advantage of their opportunities.

# Chapter 6:

*What Does Empowerment For Wealth Mean To You (How to Set Goals)*

# Synopsis

Wealth is described as the value of everything you have minus debts. A well-off person is defined as someone who's capable of living comfortably for at least five years without working.

Not every person during his lifetime may become rich, but you can be financially empowered. What does empowerment for wealth mean to you? Financially empowered is about being in control of your money, spending your finances responsibly, buying needs more often than purchasing wants and setting goals for the future.

# The Goals

Are there still lots of things you want to achieve? Do you want to become successful, but just don't know where and how to start? You might have a wealth mindset, but don't have the passion. Perhaps you keep putting your effort and time into things that are actually not useful in chasing your goals. There are many ways on how to achieve what you really want.

There's one thing that's very essential among others and once you keep wasting it, there's no way to get it back – time. If you believe that you're working hard to achieve your goals and still you're not seeing any result of your hard work, don't waste time. Instead, act quickly and try another approach before it is too late.

Did you notice how clever famous businessmen and rich people are? Through acquired expertise and hard work, they've perfected the particulars of their investments and business dealings. Once they understand they're not getting anything, they don't waste time, but instead act fast. They never stop until they find their way back in the best position and they definitely know when to react.

Negative and positive attitudes affect one's viewpoint in life. The way a person acts and interacts with people around him/her or towards a particular issue affects and reflects his/her decisions in life. Optimistic people believe in themselves, making them capable of overcoming all difficulties. To attract wealth, you should have a mental attitude that sees every good thing around you as well as makes you look forward to positive results from the actions you've undertaken to chase those goals. Positive minded people believe in their skills and don't get discouraged easily. Instead, they put more effort even after they've seen positive results. Pessimism, on the other hand, often makes people passive and scared, thus they avoid taking actions because they always anticipate the hardships, failure and disappointments it might bring.

Occasional failure should not discourage you, but it's something that you must learn from. Hardships are part of your daily life, so if you continue ranting about it, then probably you'll dwell in it forever. Successful people are determined and not afraid to stand up after every hardship. Every time they do, they always remember the important lessons they learned from all misfortunes they faced.

To have a positive attitude and wealth mindset doesn't mean that you need to be unaware of the hard facts of life. Where you come from or who you are doesn't matter as you have the capability to succeed. Have faith in yourself and learn from mistakes. Never lose your desire to achieve your goals.

# Chapter 7:
*Why Adopt The Empowerment Mindset For Wealth*

# Synopsis

Contrary to what you might have been told, there's no magical "get rich fast" system that works for every person. The only technique to build long-term prosperity is through dedication, planning and hard work. Building wealth is a long-term objective and like all long-term objectives, it starts by having the correct mindset. This goes far beyond only wishing to be rich. No one would be underprivileged if that was the case.

# Why Do It

Adopting the empowerment mindset for wealth might mean various things to different people, but usually, it boils down to determination. You have to make a plan and carry it on. It's important to determine how much of your money you can reasonably invest in an industry without going broke. You also need to reassess your plan as you lose or make money.

If you are doing well, try to invest more of your income in other valuable things. If not, you will need to cut back on some aspects. In the meantime, never take any shortcut that comes your way. These shortcuts and a steady business plan won't work. Here are some strategies to help you create a business plan.

- **Set goals**

There's no need to understand the big picture when you're just getting started. Keep it easy and simple. Set 1 year goals. What would you want to accomplish throughout the first year of your business? You can also have more goals as time passes by.

- **Decide on strategies**

To achieve the goals you have set for the company, you have to choose certain strategies to put into practice. Personal development is important to your success. You'll benefit from attending classes and discovering new strategies. Add your new found knowledge to your plan.

- **Summarize clear steps**

Once you know the strategies to apply, find out the actual steps you need to take and note them down. You have to be clear about what needs to be done and when it should be done. By being clear on what you want to accomplish, it will modify your mindset. The more you think you can attain your goals, the more likely you're to do the right actions. Also, don't forget to recognize milestones along the way. By setting your goals and tracking results, it will help you acknowledge the good things you're doing to make your thoughts a reality.

Building wealth depends on using money wisely and taking the right actions. Make sure that you're getting a good return on your investments, whether it's investing in bonds or stocks, owning real estate or building a business. Always keep in mind that adopting the empowerment mindset for wealth will help you reach your goals and live the life you have always dreamed of.

# Chapter 8:



# Synopsis

You can become empowered for wealth even during a recession. Creating a wealthy mindset involves 2 simple things – imagination and attention. By using imagination and attention, it's possible to change brain patterns to reflect that of a well-off person. How can you create a wealthy mindset?

# Doing It Right

- Think about your future.
- Feel wealthy.
- Start tithing.
- Educate yourself about money matters.
- Spend time with the rich.

## Think about your future

Visualization is a common technique that lots of people use to implement the Law of Attraction. It's a combination of imagination and attention. Spend some time regularly focusing your attention on the situation you want in your life and visualize that it's really happening. When you begin practicing visualization, you should also keep most of your attention all through the day on what you really want instead of what you don't want. A lot of people fail to do this and then question why their visualization is not working.

## Feel Wealthy

Another efficient technique for becoming empowered for wealth is to carry out things that make you feel wealthy. Think like a well-off person. How do these people think? For one thing, they don't think or say they can't afford certain stuffs. They bargain shop like everyone else, but they purchase what they want as they know they can pay for it.

Try to practice this kind of thinking by pretending you have the money you want and go on a shopping spree. Choose things that you want instead of what you think you can pay for. Then, rather than buying the items, decide that you are not going to purchase anything that day. Another way for you to do this is to try on a fur coat, plan a luxury vacation or test drive a luxury vehicle. Be sure that the activity gets you into a wealthy-thinking mode.

## Begin tithing

Tithing is an excellent way to create a wealthy mindset as you can start immediately with any amount that is comfortable. Another benefit of tithing is that it amazes your brain cells with the idea that supply is unlimited. Thinking that you have all the money to spend because more will come in is thinking profusely. It is one of the pleasures of being rich, as any well-off person will prove.

## Educate yourself about money matters

Educating oneself money matters is often overlooked, but it can be a very powerful method for becoming empowered for wealth. The more you are familiar with money matters, the more confident you'll be in handling funds. As you gain confidence to manage small amounts of cash, you'll attract opportunities to manage larger amounts of money.

As you earn more money, you'll have the knowledge needed to handle more. Or else, you won't be capable of keeping the money you attract. A lot of people attract large amounts of money, but are still near broke always because they never learned how to handle money. Don't be one of them. Educate yourself about money matters.

## Spend time with the wealthy

Spending time with well-off people can help you become empowered for wealth further. If you do not know anyone you can hang out with, look for a successful person and take him or her out to lunch. You can ask that person how he or she achieved success and what advice he or she has for others. By doing this, you will obtain a first-hand education.

If you cannot do that, then attend live seminars of successful individuals, watch their teleseminars or listen to their recorded program. There's so much available on the web. Everyone has his or her story and something important to share.

These are different ideas you can implement to become empowered for wealth. Use your imagination to create new ways and don't stop. Just believe in yourself and you can definitely do it.

# Chapter 9:
## *The Good And Bad About The Empowerment Mindset For Wealth*

# Synopsis

Wealth doesn't mean the same thing to every person. To some, being rich means having the capability to pay their mortgage or rent on time with enough money left over to treat their family or themselves to something special, while to others, it may mean having a great portfolio of assets and investments. In either case, wealth empowerment starts with a commitment to move from monetary uncertainty to monetary security.

# The Good And Bad

Wealth empowerment doesn't talk about the process of becoming wealthy, but about learning how to live within one's means and to use the existing resources to take better control of his finances and to become financially healthy and stable. What's good about the empowerment mindset for wealth? It helps you revitalize or change your thinking. If your current thinking and actions have not gotten you the monetary results that you desire, then it's time to do something completely different. To decide to change is easy, but implementing change calls for a sincere commitment.

With the empowerment mindset for wealth, you can do much more than you can possibly imagine. You can focus your thinking on changing the direction of your life to a better path and build wealth. As you already know, building wealth is not magic and if there's something bad about the empowerment mindset for wealth, it's the fact that at the end of the day, you'll still need to take action to get the luxurious life you've always wanted. The empowered wealth mindset serves as your guide in taking better control of your resources and changing your thinking to build wealth and become financially stable.

# Chapter 10:

## *Conclusion*

If you want to experience the life of the rich, believe that you're capable of building wealth. Don't easily accept your current level of wealth, thinking that great prosperity is beyond your reach. Are you struggling with the idea of seeing yourself wealthy beyond your wildest visions? Then, why don't you lower the bar and aim to simply earn extra 50 dollars per week? This is attainable for most people and will boost your confidence to think optimistically about wealth and actually build it.

Wealth will flow to people who think they deserve it and can picture themselves already in control of it. Opportunity after opportunity might come your way, but if you doubt your worthiness, you'll have a hard time building true wealth.

There might be times when the struggle is too great or seems never ending, but this is the time to persevere and remain focused on where you wish to be instead of where you are at the moment.

A simple tip that's often mentioned is to try surrounding yourself with successful and well-off people. Just being with people that you respect and possess the kind of prosperity you're striving for is a great motivator and can often create opportunities that you'd otherwise never have came across.

It's necessary to have a clear statement and vision of exactly how much wealth you want. It's no good just hoping to be affluent. Write the exact amount you're striving for and spend some time every day imagining yourself already in control of that prosperity. Feel it and get thrilled about it.

One of the main hindrances to acquiring great prosperity is limiting self beliefs. If you're harboring beliefs that you do not deserve to be rich and that having great wealth is wrong, then address these issues immediately.

Soul searching might help you. Ask yourself some questions to get rid of the negative beliefs you're holding towards wealth. Once you've cleared these emotions and thoughts, you'll be free to attract the prosperity you're entitled to.

Start your journey toward financial freedom today. It's just a matter of how you think about wealth and directing those thoughts on your end goal. Be optimistic and believe that you are worthy of it and money will come to you.